Ready Made Bouquets

Robin Lindsay Wilson

Independent Innovative International

Published by Cinnamon Press
Meirion House, Glan yr afon, Tanygrisiau
Blaenau Ffestiniog, Gwynedd, LL41 3SU
www.cinnamonpress.com

The right of Robin Lindsay Wilson n to be identified as author of this work has been asserted by him in accordance with the Copyright, Designs and Patent Act, 1988. © 2007 Robin Lindsay Wilson
ISBN 978-1-905614-27-1
British Library Cataloguing in Publication Data. A CIP record for this book can be obtained from the British Library

Designed and typeset in Palatino by Cinnamon Press. Cover design Mike Fortune-Wood from original art work generously painted for the book by Christine Woodside

Acknowledgement 'Corot's Approach to the Village of Chaville' received a commendation in the 2004 National Poetry; 'Lowry' was commended in Poetry Ealing Open Poetry Competition; 'Last Turning was awarded 3rd prize in *Poets Anonymous* seventh international poetry competition and Brancusi was placed second in *Coffee House Poetry* open competition. Other poems have been published in *Brittle Star, Aireings, Avocado, Iota, Chimera, Rain Dog, Freedom Spring, Wherever* (Cinnamon Press) *North Words, South, Cadenza Decanto* and *Carillon*.

Ready Made – an item taken out of context to become an object of art; the items are normally everyday articles, such as domestic tools, but are used in an artistic context to create a response

contents

To Alison for a world beyond words

Ready Made Bouquets

Inevitable Inventions

hope burns in my lungs
with the oxygen of spring

above my head a cloud says
this is the precise moment
you will discover penicillin

ashes fall into my shoes
and the next cloud says
with these bitter crystals
you will invent television

on the under-ripe horizon
clouds gather electricity
they say with these sparks
you will invent the telephone

I wait for the storm front
to bring me an imagination
and the gift of usefulness

I waste a lifetime watching
dark clouds approaching
with ideas tucked inside

bankruptcy is postponed
if the next thunder cloud
invents a newer explosion

a way of making it personal

Internal Architecture

next to slime on a mural wall
you wished and prayed for more
– to be born a citizen of blue sky
if you could be a citizen at all

beyond slopes of council grass
you gave up clowning to be liked
and made nothing but enemies
who encouraged you to attack

at one end of a howling arcade
you dreamed against the blast
to find the corner betting shop

the wind tore your dream away
and you cannot climb the street
until something good returns

surrender to tanned architects
who give you toy-town arches
and pink sugar-spun balconies
too small to hold an armchair
or a friend with a can of beer

surrender under buckling tiles
clinging to a concrete overhang
because you have done nothing
behind the Breezeblock screen
but procrastinate and complain

when you aspire to river luxury
and hope for mountain snow

surrender to the biting shadow
on a lonely April esplanade

remember the constant grey
above that angry tower-block
is your imagination in decay

Corot's Approach to the Village of Chaville

go down this path

a paper cut-out village
double polkas and bows
in front of your shadow

the red tiles are memories
of someone else's pleasure
but the village has no doors

the subject is the path

go down this path

a man travels with you
he whistles without sunshine
he changes your hands
takes off their idle colour
robs one victory after another

the subject is the path

go down this path

trees make your arms swing
on hollow fresh-neck days
what was the difference
between those centuries they say

the subject is the path

go down this path

there is no man with you
his eyes became afraid
when you had nothing to say
he went in the last direction
you've already been that way

the subject is the path

go down this path

after the village gate
death will make you better

it's a fear of taking my arm
it's a fear of staying here

between the hand pump
and the flyblown mule
where the noise of dry plates
and families with cutlery
reminds your eager soul

the subject is the path

Out of Order

The forest has no compass.

You are directed by pleasure,
Choosing paths of oak-light
Snaking towards adventure
And an involvement with beauty.

But the path glows infra-red
And buries itself in pine needles.
Birds switch off their song,
Romance trickles into gloom.

You realise there is no providence
Divining routes to the picturesque,
No God to create an interface
Between your petty consciousness
And this wilderness of insects
And creaking high indifference.

You need an independent truth
To keep from changing into sap,
Seed pods, tinder, Sphagnum moss,
Skeins of toadstool filaments
And tangled ancient wickedness.

The power to divide your soul
Is the contemporary temptation.

You predict the loss in silence
While panic provides a map,
An exit strategy of instant sinew
And shank bone-breath.

The inner voice wants home
Before wolves scowl from ridges
And gather a malicious strategy
To ambush your ability to reason.

When your imagination attacks,
The dogs it sends to rip the skin
Will trace your Gucci adrenaline
To every viewpoint and picnic-table.

They will quarrel over entrails,
Push bloody heads into your chest.

Your remains will wither on trees.
Your blood will darken on stones,
Then forget its belief in sunshine.

Suburban Concentration

in the minor league
there's a list of words
beyond the humdrum
discordant syllables
and car radio shout

like subatomic particles
of anti-human matter
television dialogue
falls through the fabric
of everyday soap opera

a hard word like loyalty
should not be chit-chatted
without a great silence
to wrap twice around it

it's not the age I live in
it's just the age I am

the gap between hope
and domestic achievement
is filled with sleepy sofas
and smooth little poems
– simple tabloid words

the language isn't easy

it takes wintry days
of wide awake courage
to write them down

and years of tending
to a North facing garden
to speak them aloud

Definitions: Reality

for the adored child
with the red Velcro cube
who throws the toy
to learn who the traitor is

what is real changes

for the cold grandfather
below continuing hills
watching a king depart

from the sacred smell
of soft earth in a cave
to the stink of napalm
on a girl's running skin

what is real changes

every time guns go off
every time the sun comes out
every time guests arrive
suffer your love and leave

what is real changes

you are not real flesh
until you imagine flesh

this freak's habit of suffering
is a page three photograph
this celebrity's suffering
is a story on the Internet

this neighbour's suffering
is his mistake and fate

you are not real flesh
until an iron stranger
imagines the suffering
you've almost finished
in those kicked off shoes

Integrity in Winter

old man Kuerner's too big
for the patch of snow

his bare legs stick out
his arms have folded
around the memory
of a different blizzard

he's been buried here
for decades with the wind
looking for his wise face
and the spindrift devils
thin shaving his legs
then covering him again

his crystal fine marrow
could ratchet up awake
clear-headed from death
and stagger to work
in a fug of horse breath
and undigested hay

he could wait for summer
or let another summer pass
he does not decay

the red paint is peeling
from the old wood now
sleeping doors swing
and bounce against iron
so hard the barn vibrates
and America looks out
between cracked boards

when clumps of snow
fall from a hazel branch
Kuerner has a message

his authority is a plaid shirt
with two buttons missing
his voice is clotted honey

I would rise and serve
I would rise and strive
if I heard someone speak
true and incorruptible

like the splitting of a log

Behind the Border

Ashtoreth
Chemosh
and Milcom
are dead

they were useful
but behold
they are dead

they baked their bread
made their children laugh
at uncles and injustices –
they hunted lions
but the Zidonians
and the Moabites are dead

later on the plain
where they lost a war
the Jews discovered
the old clay gods
with their heads gone

it was no loss
to those behind the border

who remembers them?

and now
Jesus
the Father
and the Holy Ghost
are dead

they were useful
but behold
they are dead

old documents were found
contradictory and incomplete
few could decipher them
but it was no loss

the English
and the Americans
are dead

after all the books
they propped up and read
to make their children laugh
now they are dead

and it was no loss
to those behind the border

who remembers them?

Jocasta

the thorny wounded man
she fought for with bracelets
rippling palm cool courtyards
embroidered shoes and scented oil
was a hard-bitten traveller

his anger sat him wide-eyed
on a damaged Persian rug
in front of the horizon

he was clever they said
saw his enemies coming

those intermittent scars
wrapping his swollen ankles
were easy mistakes to love
from the palace colonnade

yesterday bird song stopped

when his bladder was full
his family said their prayers
and watched his thin silhouette
limp into the wadi shade
to piss on cactus thorns

perhaps he'll buy them spices

today when it rained frogs
he broke a fig tree branch
and stabbed at the earth

his lever twisted the nation
turned the world modern
turned thinking outside in

when she tight-faced him
above the teetering steps
her lover was not strange

his blood-anger had shed
and he loved her innocence
with his clearest eyes

she had always told herself
who the real monster was

from the moment he was born
she controlled everything

A Barbarian on the Grand Tour

I was 19 with sunstroke
swimming in Mussolini's stadium
turning socialist-realist heads
with my flaming hair and skin

vomiting in the Youth Hostel
eating only spaghetti strands
untouched by garlic sauce
I was small and then reduced

but well enough to complain
for 2 hours on the pilgrim's train
to picture plate Michelangelo

in Florence Moses had horns
David had a saddle of fat hips

I was an unimpressed anarchist

what would have happened
if I had packed a baseball bat?

I am a wealthier cynic now
a wide U shaped belt of lard
over a baby's submerged hips

I have tried magazine advice
lost count swimming lengths
jogged to the ends of the earth

and as I spread into the future

I predict thin-faced vandals
from the impoverished country
finding wealthy city states
paintings and manuscripts

they will tear up every idea
that has not occurred to them

Divided Self

your favourite emotions
are built of concrete

your forgiven pleasures
are polished by butterflies

the ashes in your hands
are borrowed from heroes

ashes without a memory
of victories or seasons

your speech is gold-dust
your walk is starlight

there's lime and antiseptic
a scrubbed clean boundary
around each magic hand

and all the evil things
they repair and rescue
are willing and able
to hurt your children

you believe you are best
at being good and true
and God has blessed
the ignorant things you do

Beckmann

the self-portrait is mock widow's peak and blockhead
right up close in shirt sleeves and shell shocked stupidity

it's an insult to the country's heritage of Arian good looks

a new generation of self-serving critics stamp their feet
until Berlin trembles and leans from its windows to look
– the approaching jackboots grind the world into a mirror

the minor officials and over-dressed aspiring criminals
who jingle slowly and murmur along the plush ropes
have a gallery of sallow degenerates and genetic perverts
to excuse their own low foreheads and near-set eyes
there's always some sugary alien uglier than themselves

no red handed citizen will give that nasty centrepiece
a second glance or a swear word in a few years time

by then Beckmann's fake bohemian death's head stare
will pass as the true likeness of any labour camp Capo

An Actor Prepares

card tricks are easy
mind reading is tame

I can speak in tongues
even ride a water buffalo
or juggle with landmines

I specialise in rapier
on film they speed it up
but my reach is good

I'm a chainsaw artiste
the alternative circus
was my playground

in soft porn scenes
I'm a bisexual acrobat
that comes naturally

I'm able to skydive
or rip out intestines
– eat them if you want

I can pilot light aircraft
or hot air balloons
shoot poison arrows
and every kind of handgun

if you want wrestling
with sharks or crocodiles
I'm the main man

I play modern jazz
crack a stockman's whip
and walk on water
if it's a calm day

I hate myself for showing off
but it pays to advertise

if you ask me who I am
when the camera is off

if you want me spontaneous
I can act that too

Donatello

his shock is a mould
filled with lethargy
while the crowd watch
he stands like a girl

inside the mould
is disbelief
and within disbelief
there's wonder
at Goliath's head
between his feet

in his core
a hallelujah chimes
he keeps it to himself

within the secret hallelujah
there's a bedrock pause
disappointment
after victory

what will he do
when he looks
nothing like bronze
when he is clothed
beer bellied
and his children
roll their eyes
and finish sentences
in his over familiar story?

what will he do
without an enemy?

and inside the wait
for what happens next
he finds an ugly giant
who remains
unvanquished
within his sleep

and the giant
is the whole story
so huge
so shocking

David stands like a girl

Monet Bird Song

I would like to paint as the bird sings
— Monet

it is a grain stack

made strange again
by an evening
of circling sparrows
dropping snow
one crystal at a time
to teach their young
what a promise is

another bird sings

the grain stack knows
what morning is
without my song

it is Rouen cathedral

made strange again
twenty times
by a blow torch
in the hands of Christ

another bird sings

the cathedral knows
what heat is
without my song

it is a lily pond

made strange again
by petals opening
like sunspots
in the optic nerve

another bird sings

the lily pond knows
what beginning is
without my song

An X-ray of Freedom

based on the painting 'The White Drake' by Joseph Crawhall

the drake has vanished
the space keeps being free

no internal contradictions
arrowing across the pond
to be admired and fed

the gathered certainty folds
and unfolds its transparent mass
behind a fast yellow direction
until it weighs as much
as the sparkle on the water

it is only a summer thought

moving from the outer edge
of my thrown bread crumbs
towards the drifting beauty
of a simple everyday action

The Location of Remorse

based on the 1992 painting 'Young Offenders' by Stephen Campbell

the two naked young offenders
never take their solemn eyes
off the pinned down TV cops
and the offences of others

on that faithless changing screen
is everything they did before

the flickering granite faces
watch without optic nerves
the novelties of a horror film
made for Romanian television

they do not remember the kill
the kill was always repeated
when hands wore off the smell

these children have no idea
of how much torture they need
to charm muscles from their skin
or how much pain to apply
before lethargic bodies harden

they dream of football glory
and litters of Labrador puppies

neither criminal can explain
where the thought came from
to be so wicked

Lowry

hardly a wave threatening
his sweaty big black shoes

the air has been recycled
by a million tobaccoey lungs

he scoops up grey ripples
with a short handled spade
paints them better white
leaves them in a drawer

his rice-papery fingers feel
for the dancing wrinkles
in his dead mother's bed

after 10 years of watching
he does not know the steps

there is only ledger work
between tide and cloud

nobody midnight swims
nobody imagines they care

the waves he set free last year
have an iron deficiency
they will not reach the shore

perhaps early next summer
there will be more reason
to collect the rent arrears

or to row out on the pond
and watch milky ripples
try a menacing foxtrot

In the Presence of Horses

Based on Hokusai's woodblock print 'In The Horse-Washing Waterfall'

we wash ourselves
we wash the horse

I have a pain high
between my ribs
when I rinse her back

the waterfall kicks up
and shocks stars
of sun-kind skin

does the horse feel it?

forgive an old man
his summer foolishness

I should have a son
to mend the roof
bring fragrant rice
and trim my whiskers

I would teach him
how to wash a horse

my friend whistles
to pass the time

we will walk the horse
until her tail is dry

the hill grass is dying gold
the waterfall is mercury

I will remember this

Time-lapse Bouquets

based on the 1890 painting 'White and Pink Roses' by Fantin-Latour

Beauty dangling
In the curled petal,
Embracing time
And its own comfort.

Beauty overblown
Never absurd
To have bloomed,
Just commonplace.

Your gaze shifts
To prettier flowers.
You find beauty
In the budding rose
Rising from a bouquet
Of tender thorns
Fragrance and potential.

You sit too long.
I can see you fading.

And you cannot look
At the ugly truth
twisting from a filament,
about to disconnect
from summer ticking
in a smeared fruit jar.

Your hand is shaking.
Your eyes close.

I find beauty
In the wilting rose.

Last Turning

based on James Patterson's 1885 painting 'The Last Turning, Winter'

it is winter's last turn
round my shoulder blades

it's a ritual last retreat
from a stripped down country

it's barefaced me again
looping with the river
walking with my groceries
and thoughts of summer
when my hard shadow
cleared every obstacle

there's Moniaive considering
the twenty first century –
as still as a stroke of genius

there's my cold chimney
my damp buckled house

I could saunter endlessly
if I denied my heritage
and any pleasant geometry
except my own defeat

I could walk into the river
carrying these green bruises
but it would be an old lie

I must be the stranger
who decides to hesitate
and open the rough door

to lie on this pristine bed
to rise and open the shade

to feel your indifference
as if it were happening now
to any woman in the city

Love Letter

based on Ogata Karin's painting 'Pampas Grass'

just the tops of things

breezy barley heads
bouncing telephone lines

here I am
there you are

Dublin and Glasgow
both made of leaves

place your memory
in the tops of things

we were modern
a long time ago

childless unmarried
shadowless now

just the tops of things

aerials quivering
needing company

travelled light
on your anxious eyes
making my kiss

the certainty of light
on my morning hand
lifting your dream

your dream delivering
my promise to you

Brancusi

the first thing he did
was identify the kisses

this kiss is a translation
of base metal into gold
this kiss is made of airline tickets
this kiss is a gateway
this kiss is a giggle
under a thunder storm

the second thing he did
was to find the kiss' partner

beautiful back tires
kiss the cobble stones
a mind kisses a spread out body
the foreign kisses the strange

and the small things
build with single lines
all the halves of the world

the third thing he did
was to make another kiss
it only had one side
and had to be destroyed

the fourth thing he did
was to identify
who made the kiss

the kiss that all kisses imitate
the spirit kiss behind the shadow flesh
the kiss that is whole to begin with

the fifth thing he did
was to kiss himself

the sixth thing he did
was to kiss the world

The Spirit World's Guide to Self-Improvement

not yet gone and still walking
into an absence of other people

there's a gathering of spirits
in the space my chest uses

an honest ghost back-to-front
upside down and inside out
where my head used to be

I walk into his conversation
with other ghosts in café-bars
but the gap stays when rain falls
and the torn leaves scatter

I remember deciding to be born
with a stomach and a face
but the ghost and the spirits
place no trust in these things

they tell me to listen to sparks
– walk into empty public parks
– walk into empty supermarkets
– walk into empty footsteps

walk out of my emptiness
into the remains of love
in the soul of someone else

Alone Above Water

3 boats with orange sails
doing something good

and a man on board
I was too shy to watch
tie his dingy to the quay

interrupted your absence

it was all out there

being aquamarine
and half sleeping
in a tarry foreign lap
smelling diesel blossom
and faint sea-lilac

it was all out there
for us my darling

I was warm-wood happy
when I was not happy
sitting on the harbour wall

I could smell your hair
and my soul could tell
luck was coming round

Loch Fyne

for Alison

Our country is made of shingle and cloud,
its hope distributed by divisions of water.

To become citizens all we need is breath.

I breathe for my wife and she for me.

Our breath is swallowed by the loch
and held in trust by a coast of leaves
while we find good memories in silence
and a love between us answering to beauty.

When we rise from a bed of Sea Mayweed
we will find a story to last through winter.

Where the tide folds back a weight of secrets
we follow over seashells filled with light,
without petty rancour or horded loneliness,
trusting a wider sky our shadows cannot hurt
and the eternal heart beneath these waves
where the abyss sighs our souls back home.

Love Without Comfort

behind your back
on the Atlantic green sofa
my arm goes numb
but not enough
to be a stranger's arm

I can still feel
your comfort
– through another film
about the anger of Americans

and this is love
in Scotland –
this dumb arm
not waking you

A Love for All Seasons

in summer we sleep
under one thin sheet
and I fold my arms
around her bird song

my wife on a white bed
is a rowan wand
a taste of hidden rain

in autumn we sleep
under dark headlights

my wife on a white bed
is a sheaf of wheat
the sound of happiness

in winter we sleep
under plasma screens

my wife on a white bed
is a willow branch
a smell of slow river

in spring we sleep
under a child's dream

my wife on a white bed
is a handful of reeds
the sound of a tear

in summer we sleep
under one thin sheet
and I fold my arms
around her bird song

Reincarnation

there's a Celtic knot
on my married finger

and this one life

there's a sleeping ship
in this married heart

and this one life

there's a strange night
in my married eyes
kisses on my lips
repeated every day

and this one life

there's an unsteady pen
and a glass of wine
in my married hands
a good memory
when I make a fist

and this one life

there's a wishing well
in my married lap
your love song
promising enough

and this one life

there's winter boots
summer flip-flops
one more step back
into the married wish
I wore at first

and this one life

Apprentice

he works his girlfriend
from his peppery fingers
shifting cardboard boxes

her atoms stray memory
on pallets of Kitticat
fallen battered tins
of Pedigree Chum

he signs the docket
drops the steel shutter

those fat hands smell
like the world again
they belong to any man

her smell of perfume
in the fug of his room
– when she says yes
like death that yes

like running his hands
over a butcher's tray
dragging his nails
down raw heart and liver

and now it's Cat Litter
anger at the kitten on the pack
anger at this double yellow
awkward place to park –
the owner's purring face –

the other blank lad
anger bending down
reaching on tip-toes
in a poor boy's yell
of disgust and desire

not breaking sweat
this deadbeat job
is under tight control

and he dismisses it

washes his hands
in the atomic beat-beat
beat beat-beat

for the next yes girl

and his anger hides
under his fingernails
hides and touches him
like the word love

Alchemy of Trust

he can measure importance

he can pour his right hand
into clouds of hysterical wine
or crumbling base metal

his left hand is solid gold

he can look you in the eye
and hate everything you do

you do what you are told
(as little as you need to do)
and the less you achieve
the more you look like him

his eyes practice sedition
his neck is a fragile glacier
– never once surprised

he will stab you in the back
since he knows you believe
necessity tempts forgiveness

he journeys through walls
no pain can manipulate him
or transmute his arrogance
into rubies and amethysts
on the executioner's block

now you are going to learn
why you are the servant
and he is your only master

Belonging

smell my smell

it's sour jellyfish coasts
the underside of anchors
and half burnt rafters

my scent is inside
a heavy rotting net

listen to my listening

in erased landscapes
and corrected storms
along dead quarry edges
where vibrating gorse
has a new story to tell
of absentee landowners

taste my taste

it's fearless seaweed
and grey-blue shingle
it scrambles to shore
and breathes salty night
into Arisaig windows

I swim in sleep
sifting your dreams
I glide through hours
of hopes and fears
mouth opening wide

like a basking shark
history these days
is just the way I feel

you move without moving
I am moving inside you

touch my touch

feel the tide telling us
the past and the future
is this moment's pledge
that we will never leave

Where Ideas Come From

he rows her promise
beyond a reef of flies
and the secret power
of his corrupt uniform

she is tugged by a sail
invisible to soldiers
blowing the other way

his shoulders retreat
take her angry breathing
to the familiar shore

all his innocent power
takes him somewhere
he has never been before

the boat drifts to shadow
his stroke turns cold

mother and father sink
into lethargy and blame
the waves cannot decide
who should be wrecked

the baby drops his toy
and loves its return

the toy turns in the tide

daddy remembers gunfire
a perfect smoke ring
and a hot barrel smell

he used to shoot vermin
over on Three Islands

it was the scent of Eden
before she got in the way

Blessing

in the beginning
I had a laughing hill
and a double-backed kite
in Holyrood Park

I could only write
ideas with all the plot
and characters left out

now I fill in the details
with clever alcohol

I'm older now

the bad poem was the best
like your kindness
it was hot and clumsy

I was the ignorant one

between the words
and down the hill
your blessing was intimate
early morning work

the simple things
lifting me out of bed
until I disappeared
along the dreary track
to a flat roofed school

your sober blessing
was an alarm clock
set for cold and dark
with gentle fingers

when you called me
to toast and sweet tea
and money for a taxi

I was rested and ready
for my hopeless journey

Loneliness

both brick walls
border her criticism
at head height

bare saplings
empty planters
and terra-cotta vases
to complain to

it's a runway
for a toddler
not a garden

it takes her
cup after cup
of Earl Grey
to reminisce
past the poles
of the clothesline

on one side
she finds worry

the dead brown
voices of her family
in a cold-frame

at unrisen Easter
there is nothing
but chewed up grass
packets of crisps
that tip out water
by sagging daffodils

so cold clear
you could drink it

litter brings her out

she needs litter
to remember love

and tidy it

Anger Management

you're in dream trouble

blue funk in your hat
instead of adventure

thoughts could be green
singing to guiltless green

to beetles and dragonflies
if you scratched your leg
or looked into the sun

which will not take no
for a young boy's answer

mother's slapped a storm
into your locked mouth

it takes hours to tease it
petal by precious petal
into an unwilling flower

now a huff of pigment
blooms across your lips

one smile is paradise

Unpacked

Leaving is made of a turned up Hessian collar taking as long as the deserted lamp-post to rip the hairs out of a neck.

The journey is made of noticed curbs and cold dog turds.

The traveller is made of nervous chrome catches that spring without looking and fall apart when time does not speak English.

Coming back is made of sandpaper pockets worn smooth by fingertips like eye stalks on a snail.

Home is made of the old space between the cooker and the bed trampled down in days before a wish for any suitcase.

Alternative Potential

black heap in a gold clearing

it's winter smouldering in reverse
raising small orange suns
from the dead souls of leaves

it's windfall sycamore
horse-chestnut and oak this time
something more personal
smouldering underneath

a smell like the fast release
of Wellingtons or an early
discovery of damp groin
makes you sorry for people
you do not want to know

you feel like lying naked
under slimy black leaves
being smothered by winter

in the unimpressed distance
there's a nation of trees
or thoughts or dark skin

it's too far to be certain
all the branches look the same

but with a change of wind
the sorrow will leave you
you will want to see it burn

Solitude

it's too early for the mail boat
it's too late to phone my mother

it's time to listen to the rocks
to dip ripple away from myself

to watch you in the iron window
watering a dying prick of cactus
and look at the joints of water pipes
with the same amount of interest

to return to land and rediscover
what the mighty child invented –
the secret name he called himself

it's time to look at infantile waves
and the dull wink of the slipway

to notice the poisonous difference
between today's indifference
and yesterday's indifference

to be humble because it's true
not because a sulking God
kicked about by bigger boys
forgot to wear his wizard mask

but because the dripping creel
and the badly parked white van
have a space between them
where I can feel a tiny delight

Open

some villages are closed
by sneers around a chip shop

some villages are closed
by ramshackle gable-ends
and quarried grey stone

some villages are closed
by a Reo Stakis hotel
and a left over Sunday

some villages are closed
by a wrong old fence
or a bright tin shed
and a Safeway's bag
blowing across a new curb

the river Dee spreads your legs
Drumtochty Forest has no doors
the Cairngorms have no roof
or alarms and locks and keys

stop the car

some villages are closed
by the names of the dead
an over-sexed Alsatian dog
and a piecemeal bus depot

start the car

some villages are opened
by a tea-towel on the line
a flowering rhododendron
a fresh pub food sign

when we came to Ballater
the village was surrounded
by a watching spirit boundary

opened by a welcome
no one alive had built

Equinox

the Glasgow summer came
without an obvious metaphor

the smell of rubber tires
the weeds in little parks
were what they seemed to be

everything was sweating
ready to be over-stated
be loved and risk loving

lanky skip-capped van-boys
drivers labourers bin-men
were overlooked gigolos

I breezed over road works
yawned and walked away

I thought I'd found a metaphor
when the sun was in my eyes
but my shadow-self unlatched
from swollen legs and ribs

it dropped outside at noon
shapeless on the pavement

and I thought the thoughts
of a burned out flat husband

hungry and insubstantial
as you predicted me to be

I could not return or fatten
or make love until the winter

Mending Weather

the spell under the bell tower
matches your chromosomes

the structure of midday fields
is the same design as your toes

turn slowly at the crossroads
amble through the pinewoods
no cowardly shape you make
can harm this thoughtless place

if your laughter flared and fell
the tread of bracken and moss
would bounce your conscience
back to all those tiny mercies
bestowed as the country's gift

provided so many storms ago
the scars have been forgotten